SUPER STYLE

SUPER STYLE

Written by Carol Spier

Photography by Angela Coppola

LONDON, NEW YORK, MUNICH,
MELBOURNE AND DELHI

Editor Elizabeth Hester
Senior Designer Tai Blanche
Managing Art Editor Michelle Baxter
Art Director Dirk Kaufman
Publishing Director Beth Sutinis
Lead Illustrator Jeremy Canceko
Additional Illustrations Matt Dicke,
Paul Hoppe, Engly Cheng, Erin Harney
Production Ivor Parker
DTP Design Kathy Farias

DOWNTOWN
BOOKWORKS INC.

Produced by Downtown Bookworks Inc.
President: Julie Merberg
Director: Patty Brown
Editor: Sarah Parvis

Freelance Beauty Editor JoanneNoel Higgins
Photographer Angela Coppola

First published in Great Britain in 2006 by
Dorling Kindersley Limited
80 Strand, London WC2R ORL

06 07 08 09 10 10 9 8 7 6 5 4 3 2 1

A catalogue record for this book is available
from the British Library.

ISBN: 1-4053-1459-1

Color reproduction by Colourscan, Singapore
Printed and bound in China by
South China Printing Co., Ltd.

Discover more at
www.dk.com

Contents

Get ready to show your style!

Choose jewellery that's perfect for you

Pick the pieces that tie your look together

Who will you be today?

Rosie

Get ready to show your style!

Fashion accessories (and knowing how to use them effectively) can totally transform the most basic T-shirt and jeans into a look loaded with style. Style is often about the details – like what shape, colour and material something is made of, what kind of motif (like a flower or stripes) it features, and what scale it is (very big, very small or in between). The way these details are combined can create a specific look, like sporty or glam. Or the style can speak volumes about the girl who puts it together. No matter what you choose, you create an expression of your personal style every time you get dressed. So make sure your look includes lots of personality, lots of fun and lots of *you*!

Style 101

What is style? It can be a look that you see in a book, in a magazine or on TV and then recreate on yourself. Or style can be original – something that you create on your own. You can change your style often, or pick one as a signature look. Just remember these two style basics as you explore: 1) Remember that less is usually more – don't wear it all at once, even if you love it. 2) Trust your instincts – if you like the way you look, you'll communicate self-confidence!

Look at you!

What's your best look? For clues, look in the mirror. Your own features can help you find a style that's totally unique – and totally flattering. Assess your features, then watch for these icons in the book for cool style tips just for you!

Round faces like Amy's have wide cheeks and equal curves – as if the bridge of the nose is the centre of a circle. Amy also considers her light hair when picking out accessories – dark earrings really stand out.

Heart-shaped faces are widest across the forehead, with a narrow chin – like an upside down triangle. Nikki likes to balance this shape with eye-catching earrings.

Oval faces curve pretty equally above and below the cheeks, but the face is longer than it is wide. Rosie's olive-toned skin and brown hair make gold-toned jewellery a great choice for her.

Alexis has a square face, which is of nearly equal width at the forehead and jawline. With her fair, pinkish skin, she looks for rosy accessories to match.

Like Amy, Nierah has a round face. With her shorter hair, it's easy for her to draw attention to her favourite necklaces and scarves. She can also play up her dark skin with warm gold tones or bold colours.

Find your face shape

Have you ever noticed how the same pair of sunglasses can look amazing on one girl and silly on another? It's all about face shape. Did you know that accessories that contrast with your face shape are always flattering? Use this trick to find your shape, then have fun finding the best looks for you.

1 Hold your head still as you look in the mirror. Using a china marker, an inexpensive lipstick, or a bar of soap, make dots at the highest, lowest and widest points of your reflection.

2 Next, connect the dots with lines that follow your hair- and jawlines. The result is a flattened version of your face shape.

School

Wear just a few quiet, informal accessories to school; keep everything small but your book bag and maybe your watch.

Shopping

Fun, colourful things are great for hanging out with your friends or shopping. Choose a small shoulder bag to keep your hands free.

What to wear when

Accessories are attention-grabbers. Part of being stylish is knowing how to dress for different events and places. Here's a rule of thumb to help you decide: A little of anything goes almost anywhere, but a lot of it goes only certain places. For example, rhinestone studs can go to school but rhinestone chandelier earrings should not!

Out to dinner

Go for a stylish look with a belt and some jewellrry to dress up simple clothes. Carry a bag to hold your purse, comb and make up.

Fancy party

Glittery and shiny things are perfect for special parties and weddings. Don't overdo it – a few pretty things are all you need.

Choose jewellery that's perfect for you

If you love necklaces, earrings, bracelets, and rings, you've got the jewellery bug! Jewellery is a great way to finish off an outfit, add lots of personality to a look, and make your face and hands look pretty. You can totally change the look of an outfit by changing the jewellery you wear with it. In this section, we'll show what you should be thinking about when you open your jewellery box. Are you headed to a game, or out to dinner? Do you want to go for a specific look, or try something completely new? What colours and textures does your outfit have? Once you see how to choose the pieces that are right for you, you'll be ready to step out in style!

Studs & drops are simply stylish

Studs are the simplest earring style – a front decoration mounted on a post (for pierced ears) or a clip (for non-pierced ears). Drops are a little longer – they hang just below your earlobes. Both are great for chic, small-scale style that can go anywhere. And there's a wide variety of styles – from plain to sparkly to whimsical. Choose a colour that matches part of your outfit, or if your outfit is all one colour, pick a strong contrast for your ears. Or go with gold or silver – they look nice with everything.

Pretty and petite

Because studs are small, they never compete with the rest of your outfit – it's fine to wear a pair that glitters with casual clothes. Earlobes are different sizes, so experiment to see what size stud looks right on you.

style tip
If you want your earrings to really stand out, pick a pair that contrasts with your hair colour – dark earrings for blondes or light ones for brunettes.

Small and delightful
Coloured drops are sweet peeking out from under long hair. Earrings in bold colours can stand alone so go without a necklace to draw all the attention to your ears.

These spiky little fuzzballs are super-light, so your lobes will be in the pink.

Pick faceted gems to set off your eyes – blue for blue or green eyes, green or amber for brown eyes.

Mini-size, mega-style

Whimsical shapes show your sense of humour – here Black Kitty sports a tiny pink bow.

Every diva loves diamonds – triangle studs add a pretty sparkle to your smile.

Keep your spirits light and summery with super-cool wire-wrapped stone drops.

Hearts always say "sweet". Wear faceted drops like these for dressy dinners or parties.

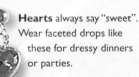

Be dashing with dangles & hoops

Dangle and hoop earrings are splashy and fun. The bigger and jazzier they are, the more attention they call to themselves – so wear them when you really want to show your style. They look especially cool with short hair; if your hair is long, you'll look more sophisticated in dangly earrings or big hoops if you pull your tresses back.

Swing low
Your dangles should hang freely from your ears. If they're so long they drag on your shoulders, they look silly, not cool. Pick a length that swings free.

style tip

If your face is round, try square or star-shaped hoops for a cool contrast.

In the loop

Round, oval, or crescent-shaped, hoops come in many sizes. A size that hangs above or below — not at — the corner of your jaw is most flattering.

Large plain hoops are the ultimate basic! This gold pair look sporty.

Big on glamour

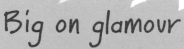

Small hoops go anywhere. Break away from the classic solid-metal version with this trendy beaded pair.

Catch the light with long, lean dangles ending in pearly pink drops.

Gypsy discs and funky beads give these chandeliers a bohemian flair.

Clips, springs and magnets

Pierced earrings look great but you don't have to have your ears pierced to wear pretty earrings. If you do pierce, be sure to have it done by a professional and follow the ear care instructions for keeping your holes clean until they heal. If you don't pierce, there are plenty of other ways to wear all kinds of great earring styles. Try cute magnetic studs or clip-on dangles – these cool styles are designed to look like the real thing with none of the hassle!

Faux pierced earrings

Magnetic charm. Hold stud earrings on your ears with tiny magnets placed on the back of your earlobes. They look exactly like studs for pierced ears!

Spring into place. Hinged earrings like these hoops open so you can put them on, then close to clasp your earlobe. The hinge hardly shows.

Slide to secure. These cute hoops have pretty beads for a glam touch. They stay on with a spring-loaded clasp.

style tip

Clip-ons can slip off-centre a little, so check every once in a while to make sure they're where you want them.

A design like this star in two circles is both delicate and bold.

A cascade of tiny stars brings the Milky Way right to your ears.

Eye-foolery

Your ears look pierced with these clip-on dangles. They feature just enough ornament at the front of the earlobe to conceal the hinged clasp and they're as pretty as real pierced styles.

Necklaces: short & sweet

Whether choker or chain, a short necklace can be long on style options. With a T-shirt or round neck sweater, make sure your necklace is bigger than the shirt neck and hangs easily over it. If you're wearing a blouse with a collar, put the necklace inside – you won't see as much of it, but it will make a pretty accent.

Short styles

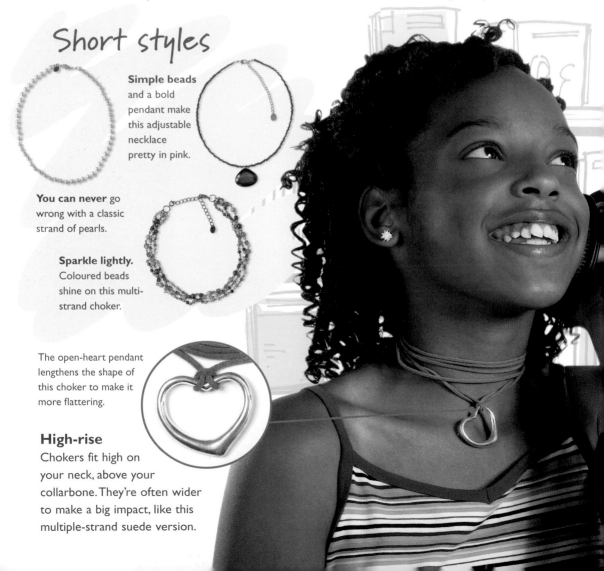

Simple beads and a bold pendant make this adjustable necklace pretty in pink.

You can never go wrong with a classic strand of pearls.

Sparkle lightly. Coloured beads shine on this multi-strand choker.

The open-heart pendant lengthens the shape of this choker to make it more flattering.

High-rise

Chokers fit high on your neck, above your collarbone. They're often wider to make a big impact, like this multiple-strand suede version.

Find your ideal necklace length

What's the most flattering length for a necklace? The length that echoes the curve of your face. Here's how to find it.

1 Look in the mirror and find the widest part of your face. Trace the shape your jawline makes from that point. You can use lipstick to draw it on the mirror.

focal point

A simple strand of beads is just that much prettier with a special pendant. Some necklaces come with pendants, but you can usually add one when they don't.

2 Put on a necklace and adjust its length so it follows that line. Stand on a step stool to match the line on the mirror.

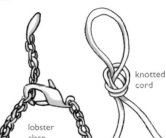

knotted cord

lobster clasp

3 Once you've found the length you like, clasp the necklace. Chain necklaces usually have an adjustable clasp so this is easy to do. To shorten a ribbon- or cord-style necklace, try tying a small knot behind your neck.

This flower pendant fills the hollow of your neck in a pretty way.

Necklaces: long & lovely

Long strands of beads make strong style accents; the chunkier they are, the more attention they grab. However, you do want to be sure that the length isn't overwhelming. Here are two good ways to wear long necklaces.

Tie a knot

Put on a very long strand of beads and tie it in a loose slip knot somewhere below your collarbone; let the rest dangle lower like a tassel. You can also try tying two strands together for a funkier, chunkier look.

Slide the knot so it sits at your ideal short necklace length to draw focus up toward your face.

Slide the knot lower on your chest so the top of the necklace makes a V – this elongates your look.

style tip

To change an ordinary necklace into one that's super-long, use a co-ordinating bracelet or ribbon – or just clasp two similar-looking necklaces together for a look that's twice as nice!

Wrap in loops

Loop a really long strand several times around your neck and adjust so each wrap sits at a different level. You can add or subtract wraps to get the best look for you.

Super-long beaded strands work well in this look. Try twisting two together to bring lots of colour to your neck area.

Show your colours

A silver chain with geometric silver beads reflects pretty light onto your face. This delicate style looks striking with a simple outfit.

Gold-toned metallics shed a warm glow. The dangling discs on this pretty necklace will glimmer as you move.

Brighten up. Choose colourful beads that match or contrast with your outfit. Beads in several sizes on wire links make this strand especially pretty.

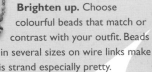

Style a necklace combo

Layering necklaces is one of the coolest ways to personalise your look. These combos look especially good with tops that have wide necklines or skinny straps. Plus, they're a great excuse for raiding your jewellery box! Just remember these rules of the road: Try to find pieces that have something in common, and layer them so they fall at different lengths. Got it? OK, girls – start your combos!

Layer with flair

Create a necklace combination that is right for your size – you want it to flatter your face, not outshine it. Taller girls can wear chunkier strands than shorter girls.

1 Choose one necklace to be your "foundation" and put it on. It can be colourful, quiet or sparkly, bold or delicate, or have a pendant or locket. You can double a long necklace to be the foundation.

2 Put on other necklaces with a colour or material in common with the first. If they have a similar look, they will look like one piece of jewellery. If not, they will look more dynamic. Both options work.

3 Arrange the necklaces to lie smoothly, in concentric loops. If a longer one has a pendant, or if you want to tie it in a knot to give it importance, make sure it hangs free of the other necklaces.

Master the mix

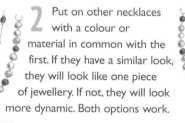

Cast a spell in stacked chain and leather chokers. Add a throbbing heart and dangling faux bone – so cool.

Walk the beach in strands of white and watery blue. Shell beads, knotted cord and a palm tree design tie up the nautical theme.

Step lightly in a cascade of delicate silver chains. Arrange them so the pendants hang in order from small to large.

style tip

Your layered combo is just one part of your look. Get dressed before you put on your necklaces so you can see the full effect with your outfit.

Balancing act

For the prettiest effect, mix necklaces that are slightly different in scale, like these, where the number, size, and spacing of the beads varies. The pink, white and silver colours balance each other so none of them comes off too strong.

Earrings & necklaces for every day

When you're putting together an everyday look, don't worry about matching pieces exactly – just pair things that go with your outfit and have a similar type of look. For instance, pink goes with pink, silver goes with silver, funky goes with funky. Here are some tips to help you strike a balance that's right for you.

My face is square, so I go for longer necklaces and earrings that hang either above or below my jaw.

I like to pair V- and Y-shaped necklaces with smaller earrings – they balance each other and flatter my round face.

My oval face looks different when my hair is up, so I choose my jewellery after I do my hair.

Match the proportions

To make your style look consistent, pick earrings and necklaces with the same kind of style impact. Pair delicate earrings with a delicate necklace, or match chunky with chunky – aim for similar "visual weight".

Match the material

When your earrings and necklace are
made with the same materials (metal,
shells, glass) in the same finish (shiny or
dull) they go together naturally, even If
they're not really a set. The beads
in these earrings match those
in one of the necklaccs.

Earrings & necklaces for special occasions

For dressy times, it's fun to wear sparkling, festive jewels. Just keep in mind that a little glitter next to your face has a big impact. It's easy to go overboard. When in doubt, stay on the lighter side and choose a necklace and earrings that bring out your prettiest features — your eyes and your smile.

Long-ish, sparkly earrings really dress up my heart-shaped face; I like them with short glittery necklaces.

I love to wear chandelier earrings and glittery chokers for dress-up — they're pretty with my oval face.

I like to balance my round face with long beads tied in a knot and cool cascade earrings or super rhinestone studs.

Choose a hue

Pick a colour theme for your necklace and earring combo – match your dress or eyes or go for your favourite tint. These clear and blue crystal beads go well with the model's blue flower hair accessory.

Material theme

Rhinestones send out rays of dancing light. Try small droplets like these – at your ears and ringing the base of your neck – as a sparkling frame for your face.

I ♡ earrings!

Don't forget to:

1) Find earrings for Aunt Jane's wedding

2) Pick out jewellery for lunch with Grandma

3) Shop for a cool pair of summer earrings

4) Finish organizing earring collection!

So pretty

1

2

3

4

5

For my birthday?

6

7

The whole team should get these.

8

9

10

11

12

Perfect with my new dress!

13

14

Wish List

1 Seahorse drops
2 Gold disc cascades
3 Playing card studs
4 Bead drops
5 Flat square hoops
6 Flip-flop posts
7 Heart & chain cascades
8 Cool curly hoops
9 Teeny cherry posts
10 Basketball studs
11 Dangly star hoops
12 Heart-shape hoops
13 Pink rhinestone studs
14 Green frog drops
15 Bohemian dangles
16 Flower bead hoops
17 Hanging dice dangles

15

16

17

Favourite necklaces

Your favourite necklace may change year by year, season by season or even outfit by outfit, but these classic designs have a gift for style that's good for the ages. With these pretty choices, you'll have great looks wrapped up, no matter what the occasion!

Gold locket

Pink pearls

Side-hung heart pendant

Gem chain

Rhinestone pendant

Chunky silver chain

Beaded wire with pendant

Beaded choker

Colourful thread wraps

Mixed glass beads

Silver beads

Disc pendant

Coloured stone pendant

String of silver stars

Wooden beads

Shells on knotted cord

Here a pin, there a pin

Pins, badges and brooches are a cool and versatile way to make a simple outfit look special. They can go on the shoulder of a jumper, near the neckline of a blouse or right below a skinny strap. A really large pin, like a fabric flower, can make a big statement on its own — but there's no rule that says you have to stop with just one!

Make a pin cluster

A grouping of pins looks great on a lapel or pocket. Start by picking a theme, like "things from the garden" or "smooth metal", then have fun finding ways to express it.

1 Start with a group of your favourite pins. They should have some theme in common: colour, motif or material. Place the largest pin first.

2 Add a smaller pin next to the first. Make sure the pins don't stick out over the edge or over the lapel fold.

3 Add more pins, arranging them so they look good to you and fill the lapel pleasingly. There isn't a rule for doing this — it depends on the shape of the pins.

style tip

Did you ever lose a pin? If you insert the prong from top to bottom, it won't fall out so easily if the clasp comes open.

Pin points

Want to make a big statement on a simple outfit? Try wrapping a ribbon or long scarf around your waist like a belt — or thread it through your belt loops — then use one big pin or a group of little ones to secure it.

Remember, the bigger the scarf, the bigger the pin should be – a tiny pin will get lost on a broad scarf.

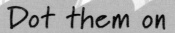

Dot them on

Flutter by – pretty insect pins are as colourful as the real thing but they hold still and won't sting!

Pin up your favourite faces with mini-portraits of movie stars, pop star or favourite causes.

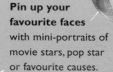

Glitter into style with a big brooch of faceted gemstones.

Rules of the wrist

It's temping to just throw on your favourite bracelet without even thinking but as with any accessory, the trick to looking really polished is to work with all the other parts of your outfit. With bracelets, that means sleeves, especially. Consider these tips for getting the look right: 1) The more arm that shows, the more bracelets you can wear. 2) Shirt cuffs rule – pick bracelets big enough to fit over them or hang free of them, or small enough to slide inside them. Here are five winning combos.

With a blazer…
Links, with charms if you like, are a great choice – just don't wear anything glittery unless it's a dressy jacket.

style tip
I find it really distracting when people wear jangling bracelets in school or church or any place I need to concentrate – so I test the noise factor of my bracelets before I leave the house.

With wide or loose sleeves…
Wear one big bracelet – or a cluster that looks like one. Loose bangles are good if you wear several at once.

With a denim jacket...

Pick something chunky. Try a couple of big bead stretch bracelets, a cuff or something with a big dangle. Textured materials like wood, leather, cord or embossed metal look cool too. Bright colours grab the eye!

With a cuffed shirt...

Go with one bracelet, either tight and not bulky or loose enough to ride over the shirt cuff, like a bangle. To add some attitude, turn back the cuffs – you'll look casual and the world will get a better look at your bracelets.

With short sleeves or no sleeves...

Wear as many bracelets as you like, but unless you're really trying to make a statement, don't let the total get wider than the distance from your wrist to the inside base of your thumb.

Style a bracelet combo

Every time you put together a great arrangement of bracelets, you're demonstrating your fashion flair. It's all about experimenting and expressing personal style. Here are two hints to get you started: First, choose bracelets that have some common element, like colour or material. Then look at yourself in a full-length mirror – this is a trick designers use to see their work from a distance, the way other people will see it.

Stack them up!

style tip

An otherwise simple outfit is the perfect fashion opportunity for lots of bracelets – a plain background will offset whatever you have going on around your wrists.

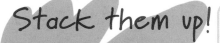

Rock your style with bracelets in patent leather and metallic details. This set follows a theme of pink, black and starry motifs.

This beachy set follows a colour theme closely for an overall effect that's bold but not too wild.

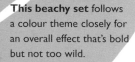

Ride the range with a belt-style cuff and beaded leather bangles. Desert hues set the tone and mix well with Western styles.

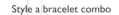

Mix, match and layer

The things the bracelets are made from (glittery gems, polished stone, tumbled stone, plastic, shell, wood, leather etc.) have as much to do with your combination's success as the type of bracelets you combine. Choose materials that together look dressy, sporty, funky, casual or whatever expresses the style of your outfit.

1 First, gather the bracelets you want to combine. Then pick one bracelet as your base. It's easiest to begin with something big, like a set of stretch beads, skinny bangles, or chunky beads. Put it on your wrist.

2 Add another bracelet or a set of skinny ones. Pick something that's different from the base piece but has something in common with it, too – like colour or material.

3 Add one more bracelet or another set of skinny ones. Again, pick something that's different from the others but has something in common with them – or choose something in the same design but in a different colour.

Keep your rings in character

What do you think about when choosing a ring to wear? Extra-large and glittery rings are real attention grabbers; they're great for fancy events – but don't forget to keep your nails nice. For everyday wear, your best bet is small rings that don't get in the way. No matter what you choose, be sure your ring reflects the person you are – or at least the person you want to be today!

Personality plus

Dreamy poet: Grace your finger with a set of several slender, muted metal bands with small stones. Faceted gems are fascinating.

Outgoing and lively: To invite conversation, wear a really big "cocktail" ring with lots of commanding sparkle.

Talented artist: Sleek sculptural shapes show your individual flair. Pick a style with a motif that reflects your take on what's truly cool.

Quiet but strong: Keep it simple – choose a delicate band with a few small stones in a plain setting.

Cool sophisticate: Slide on a set of sleek, smooth, matching bands, each set with a single small stone. Let them twist as they will.

History lover: Choose a retro or old-fashioned style. Metal with stones is romantic.

style tip

Want to keep ring settings from snagging your clothes? Try painting them with clear nail polish. Check first, to be sure the ring isn't valuable.

Team captain: Pick a colourful, sporty style that looks fuss-free and assertive. Stay away from faceted stones.

Head of the class: Be classic with a class ring! These rings look fancy but they're perfect to pair with school clothes or weekend wear.

Totally confident

A big faceted gem looks super sophisticated. Wear this kind of ring when you want to be noticed!

A great sense of fun:
Whimsical shapes like musical instruments, animals, or insects make people smile.

Time for style

Watches are a cross between jewellery and practical gear, giving you a stylish way to keep an eye on the time. They're a lot like bracelets – some styles are simple and pretty enough to be worn anywhere but watches that are definitely sporty or especially fancy belong with the appropriate look. When you're deciding what goes with what, think about the design of the face as well as the band.

Buckle-up
The extra straps and hardware lend pizzazz to a classic, tailored watch.

style tip
Take a look at your watch face. If it looks scratched, you may be slamming your hands around more than you realize. Take a tip from your watch and try to be more graceful with your hands.

Swing time
Charm-style watches masquerade as delicate bracelets. Choose one on a stripy pastel ribbon band for a feminine accent.

Wrist wrap
Scarf-style or soft ribbon bands are certainly very girly – but how dressy they are depends on the fabric used and the style of the watch itself. Be sure to tie the knot very securely.

It's a guy thing

A big watch makes your wrist look delicate. Choose an heirloom style or something totally modern – this one has a cool spinning top with rhinestones!

Watch the time

A fabric band with Velcro closure, together with a jeweleld watch case creates an everyday watch with lots of sparkle.

Flip top

The snap-up cover over the face of this digital ring-watch is perfect for sporty girls.

Wide leather bands like this one work best with daytime looks that are tailored, smart or sporty,.

Sweet heart

Pretty as a bracelet, this heart-shaped watch on a slender metal band is feminine but not at all fussy – wear it with jeans and t-shirts, or with skirts and dresses.

Long face

High-design types may prefer the sleek lines of a rectangular face. A coloured dial keeps it from being too serious.

A watch that's meant to fit loosely (like a bracelet) with a delicate link or chain band works best when you're dressed up.

Hands-on style

You know how to choose rings, bracelets and watches – what about putting them all together? Just remember this rule of thumb – hand jewellery draws attention away from your face, so be conscious of how your overall look will be impacted. Ready to try your hand at an ensemble? Here are some ideas to get you started.

Make an impact

Pick a chunky bracelet and watch and put them on one hand only. Make them the same colour, matching a colour from elsewhere in your outfit. Choose a ring with that colour too.

To keep my long fingers from looking skinny I like to wear several delicate rings on one finger.

I think my small hands look best with one delicate ring and either a watch or a bracelet, but not both.

Cool combo

When you want to wear something on each wrist, choose pieces that are low-key and have something in common – like these pearly pink beads and silver watch with pink face.

Decorate Your tootsies

When it's flip-flops-and-sandals weather, put on a toe ring or an ankle bracelet – or both – to jazz up your feet. The rings can go on whichever toe you like (or as many toes as you think look cool). Here are four ways to co-ordinate flip-flops and foot jewellery.

Twinkle, twinkle
Jewel-trimmed flip-flops make feet sparkle. Let them take centre stage and add delicate toe rings and anklets.

style tip
Wearing an ankle bracelet may feel weird at first. You may need to get used to wearing one.

Summer blooms

Co-ordinates are cute. Pair a string of teeny flower beads with bold flower trimmed flip-flops. Add matching beaded toe rings for even more flower power.

Mix it up

Opposites attract so don't be afraid to pair sturdy sandals with delicate jewels. Here a wrap-style toe ring has just the right weight, and a shimmery finish ties it all together.

Gang them up

Wear a couple of anklets in the same theme. A striped canvas strap on the flip-flops calls for a casual, beachy look. How about a toe ring in the shape of a flip-flop?

Hair accessories

Heads up, girls! You put a lot of effort into looking great – don't sell you style short by just picking the first clip or ponytail elastic that comes to hand. Instead, choose your outfit and then pick hair accessories for style and colour just as carefully as you do the rest of your jewellery. Whether they reinforce your look in a subtle way or steal the show with a bold piece, hair accessories truly top off your style.

Smart match

Choose larger hair accessories like headbands in a style that goes with your outfit – don't mix a sparkly band with sweatpants! For a low-key look, match the band to your hair colour.

A comb with this much sparkle is a great way to make a simple style simply gorgeous!

Key item

To make a big style statement, use an important hair accessory like a glittery comb, big flower or colourful bow as your primary accessory.

Tress dress-up

Use twisty ponytail elastics to put the prettiest grip on long, flyaway locks. Pick colours that match your outfit. Use more than one!

Put fancy slides in your hair to add surprise to a simple outfit. Even the very shortest cuts can find a spot for one or more of these.

Girls with long tresses are lucky – these hair sticks bring an exotic touch to simple up dos, and keep them neat, too.

Art for your body

Temporary body jewellery is funky and fun – and best of all, you can change it whenever you're ready for a new design. There are two main types of body art – temporary tattoos and self-sticking gems. Both come in packages with suggested designs, but you can also combine them in any way that suits your fancy. Just be sure to read the packaging carefully to find out how to use them properly, and ask an adult to give their OK before applying them to your skin.

style tip

Temporary tattoos last about a week, so check your calendar before you commit!

Jewellery artist

Use temporary tattoos and self-sticking gems to create a piece of jewellery, right on your skin. Create an unusual necklace, bracelet or cuff with temporary tattoos. Then use the gems to accent your favourite parts. Cute!

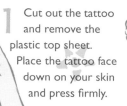

1 Cut out the tattoo and remove the plastic top sheet. Place the tattoo face down on your skin and press firmly.

2 Dip a sponge or cloth in water and rub it on the back of the tattoo until the paper backing is evenly damp.

3 Wait 30 seconds Peel off the backing. Rinse the tattoo gently. Let it air dry.

Stick them on

Glitter-and-glow cherries are perfect summertime accents.

Choose exotic curled shapes or fancy butterfly outlines in black for a bohemian effect.

Let a school of colourful dolphins swim around your ankle or down your arm.

mix and match

Use a mix of body gems and temporary tattoos to decorate your upper arm, your calf or any other spot large enough to feature more than one motif.

Treasures for hands and feet

If you were stranded on a fashionable desert island, which accessories would you need? Whatever your treasured pieces are, they're bound to attract attention. Whether you go funky, dressy, casual or just everyday cool, pick bracelets and watches thoughtfully to complement your outfit and your personal style.

1 Multi-strand
   bracelet
2 Glam watch
3 Beaded stretch bracelets
4 Silver bangle
5 Funky bead bracelet
6 Pretty shell bracelet
7 Classic pearl bracelet
8 Pink gem ring
9 Dangly cherries toe ring
10 Filigree ring
11 Brown bead toe ring
12 Blue beaded ring
13 Funky plastic ring
14 Dolphin ring
15 Double-band ring
16 Deather butterfly ring
17 Silver butterfly ring
18 Beaded toe ring
19 Dangling disc anklet
20 Pearl-and-stars anklet
21 Glass bead anklet
22 Turquoise cuff watch
23 Square silver cuff watch
24 Cute polka dot watch
25 Ribbon-strap watch
26 Brown bead anklet
27 Knotted cord bead anklet

Spice it up

Give a surprise finish to your style by adding a pretty hair ornament, a cool body jewel, or a super pin. To see things on the back of your hairdo, face away from a big mirror and look into a hand-held mirror.

16

17

15

14

13

1 Decorative slides and hair pins make hair shine with style.

2 A twist-in flower is makes a subtle centrepiece for updos.

3 This rhinestone sparkler looks pretty on all hair types.

4 Plastic mini-crocodile clips are casual favourites.

5 Shiny metallic mini-clips dress up or down with ease.

6 Hair sticks and vertical clips hold a hair twist with flair.

7 Square clips have a cool edge.

8 Bright flower slides are super-festive!

9 This funny fuzzy brooch makes a statement.

10 Jade-coloured petals make this flower brooch look smart.

11 This brooch has feathers and gems and beads – oh my!

12 This chic square pin gives bird lovers a good name.

13 A jewelled dragonfly looks classic on a lapel.

14 This beachy flower brooch is at home on a summery outfit.

15 Tiny earrings can double as pins.

16 Body gems are gorgeous!

17 Temporary tattoos are even cooler in a sparkly finish.

10

11

12

Nierah

Rosie

Amy

Alexis

Pick the pieces that tie your look together

Bags, hats, scarves, belts, gloves and sunglasses are great style changers. When you wear them, you're not only styling an outfit, you're doing what fashion pros call "extending your wardrobe". By giving basic clothes different looks, these accessories are a great way to refresh a favourite ensemble or polish the look of special outfits. So how do they work for you? Do you wear a variety of styles or stick with a few that give you a signature look? Do you like to make a big statement or use accessories to tie together your look in subtle ways? Whatever your style, this section will help you make the right accessories choices for you.

Put big bags to work

When you've got lots to carry, stash it in a large bag. Generous backpacks, shoulder bags and large totes are the bags to choose when you're carrying a large load. Pick the type that works best for each purpose — messenger bags can be a nice change from a backpack for school books or sports gear; a compact backpack may work just as well for shopping (think hands free!) as it will on a hike in the woods.

style tip

When you're wearing a big backpack or shoulder bag you need to pay attention to who or what's behind you — you don't want to bump a wide load into your friends.

Stash and carry

Tote style shoulder bags are easy to get things in and out of. And things that don't fit exactly (like an umbrella) look OK sticking out of the top. If you stash lots in a soft tote, check the mirror for bulges that look messy. And keep in mind — totes don't offer much security from prying hands or the weather, so pick one with an inside zipper pocket for your wallet.

Pick your style!

Make a splash – watery blues send this stripy tote to beach, pool or anywhere else you want to look and feel cool.

Take a stroll – straw is perfect for summer outings. Leather trim and flower appliqués are sweetly sassy.

Carry a "conversation" print – pick a tote patterned with things you love, like these shoes and bags.

Wide straps keep you comfy when you're carrying a big bag – especially when it's filled to the brim.

The big easy

A big tailored shoulder bag is more sophisticated and not so bulky as a backpack, and you can get lots into it. This kind of bag is great for papers and notepads and things you want to keep flat. Piped pockets with grommets and D-rings add pizzazz to this purple corduroy example.

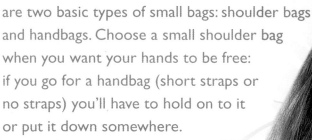

Small bags travel light

You'll always look pulled together if you pare your carry-along gear to the minimum essentials so it fits in a smallish bag. There are two basic types of small bags: shoulder bags and handbags. Choose a small shoulder bag when you want your hands to be free: if you go for a handbag (short straps or no straps) you'll have to hold on to it or put it down somewhere.

style tip

Try tying the straps of a small shoulder bag in a bow to turn it into a handbag.

Sleek sophisticate

Small shoulder bags are neater than big ones, and still give you hands-free carrying. Leather in a pretty colour with a flap and buckle closure is right for almost any occasion.

Get a grip

Hit your stride with a small zip-top shoulder bag — star trimmed leather pairs well with both jeans and skirts.

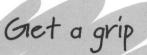

Bright clutches like this pink and green daisy design **work** great alone or can also be slipped into larger bags as organizers.

Tiny beaded styles are sophisticated— great for times when you really want to dress up.

Neat and trim

For a classic, pulled together but casual look, choose a cloth handbag with outside pockets. Tweedy fabric trimmed with a bow is super chic.

Clip on a fancy key ring for added fun.

Pick brims for sunny days

Brimmed hats have lots of character. When you're choosing one, tilt it at several angles to see the effect and try your hair different ways too. Brimmed hats in straw or canvas are perfect for sunny days, but wool or felt versions are great for winter, too – they'll help keep in the heat and keep the snow out of your face.

On or off the range

Cowgirl hats are fun to wear; they can be tilted to the side, the brims can be rolled and they come in lots of colours and materials. Jeans and t-shirts are an obvious match for a cowgirl hat, but tiered skirts look pretty cool too.

Pick your style

A bucket hat shades your eyes. Cute versions like this are great for boating, walking or hanging out.

This wide-brimmed hat has a tallish crown (the top part) and a splashy 60's-print for fun.

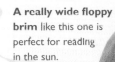

A really wide floppy brim like this one is perfect for reading in the sun.

Classy classic

A sleek cloche, with a small down-turned brim that flares ever so slightly, takes its name from the French word for bell. Wear this style pulled almost straight on your head, not tilted too far to the back or the side.

Caps for all seasons

Caps – brimless styles and those with peaks or earflaps – can be cool and cosy. There are funky styles with attitude, styles that keep you warm and others that shield your eyes from the sun. Even if you think they absolutely "make" your outfit, most caps belong off indoors – the exception is a summery one that's knit or crochet, which you can leave on all the time. Arrange or tilt your cap to find the angle you like best.

Pick your style!

Peaked caps come in different proportions. Test them to see whether you like the bigger or smaller scale best.

Some knit caps cover your ears and others don't. Pull them down on your forehead, then experiment to choose a straight or curved line above your eyes.

Baseball caps are always fun, and a great way to keep the sun off your face.

Snow cosy

Snuggly warm insulated caps – the kind with a cuff and earflaps – tend to make your head look bigger. Don't fight it, just play along and choose one that's colourful or has cute details like pompom ties.

Crafty stuff

Handmade looks are cool for caps. Whether crochet, like this one, or knit colourful yarns make you smile at winter gloom.

style tip

Wear a hat you feel comfortable in – if it makes you feel stylish, you'll communicate confidence. If it makes you feel silly, go without.

Trim it up

You probably don't change your bag every day, so it makes sense to choose one that really reflects your style. And then why not add a flourish to personalise it, either to match an outfit or keep it distinct from other girls' similar bags? You can add jewellery, a scarf or some ribbon, or, if you like to do crafty projects, you could add painted designs or cool appliqués (ask an adult first if that's okay). Here are some ideas to try.

A big soft fabric flower pin will look especially nice on a fabric bag.

Make your bag special

There are lots of ways to add pizzazz to a bag. Cloth and straw bags are easier to embellish than leather or plastic ones, because you can pin into them without hurting them – but you can safely tie things onto the handle of any bag.

1 First look at your jewellery and scarf collection to see what would make a cool accent. Pick things that look nice with your bag.

Show off a favourite pin by placing it prominently on your bag. This sparkly pin really catches your eye.

More super style

This polished stone brooch has the sophisticated look of jade in a playful design.

This scarf has silver threading to add interest and a touch of shine to your bag.

A colourful butterfly brooch looks pretty on a bag or a shoulder.

A square pin can be centred on a pocket to look like part of the original bag design.

2 Add your accent choices: Tie a scarf around the handle, place a pin on the pocket or flap or both.

A silky scarf tied onto the bottom of a strap looks casually elegant. Double it up for a shorter, pouffier look.

Pick sunglasses with flair

Your choice: make a big statement with big glasses, or be more low-key. If you're picking small glasses, shapes that make a contrasting angle on your face are a sure bet, but frames that repeat your face shape show lots of attitude. Pick colours that match your hair or contrast it for fun, or choose colours that match your outfit. Try on the biggest pair you can find – it's fun when glasses dominate your face.

style tip

Unless your hair is really short, try on sunglasses and see how they look with your hair both loose and pulled back.

Fly away

Aviator glasses (like these, with two bars across the bridge of your nose) suggest adventure. Cool candy colours make them girly. Check different pairs to find your best look – shapes vary.

Look the look

Wraparound glasses cup the sides of your face and hide more of your eyes. The ones shown here are rimless, but you'll find plenty with pretty and colourful rims too.

Cat's eye frames have a slanted, almond shape that makes wearers look cool and sophisticated. Some pairs have a more exaggerated shape than others.

Go glam. Movie-stars-to-be will get a boost from retro styles worn by divas of the past. These slightly chunky, squarish shapes look great paired with ponytails or head scarves.

Square off

Square frames look cool on almost everyone. Try on slender wire frames as well as thicker plastic ones to see which scale looks best. Go for a bright colour to make a strong statement!

Hats and shades

Here are some tips for picking hat and sunglass combos:
Big brims usually call for lighter weight frames while caps
work well with larger frames. Small brims and peaks
work with either. It's easy for your features to
be overwhelmed, so check the effect in the
mirror. If you like what you see – wear it!

Hit the streets

Peaked caps are cute and snappy. Pair
them with delicate frames – granny
glasses, frameless tinted glasses, semi-
wraparound types and wire aviators
all look cool.

A small brim hat and delicate cat's eye frames look best on my round face.

Wider brims and frames keep my oval face from looking long. I'm cool in most large frames.

My face is square so I go for diagonals — angled brims and upswept frames.

To contrast the top of my heart-shape face, I tilt my hats and wear small frames.

Take the reins

Cowgirl and other big hats have lots of style — wear them with quieter frames that are not too decorated, like wrap-arounds or understated classic oval shapes. Stay away from aviator or cat's eye frames — they have so much style they'll compete with the hat.

Go that extra fashion mile

Long scarves have tremendous personality, which they'll happily lend to whatever outfit you wear them with. Tie them on your head, around your neck, around your waist and hips — different fabrics give different effects, so be creative. Use a bright or patterned scarf to jazz up a plain top or a plain scarf to tone down a busy outfit. You can never have too many scarves!

Heads-up on scarves

A classic way to wear a long scarf is wrapped around your head. This flattering style frames your face in a pretty way while it keeps hair back. It can be tricky to get the knot and placement right, so ask a friend for help if you need to.

1 With hair pulled back out of the way, wrap a long scarf around your head like a headband. Place it over or under your ears as suits your look. If the scarf is too wide, fold it or pleat it to make it narrower.

2 Tie the ends together in a knot with streaming tails. Experiment to see if you like the tails at the base of your neck or above or below one ear. Then fix your hair in a ponytail or let it hang loose.

Easy does it

Breezy cotton stripes make a cool
head wrap that looks sleek with the
ends hidden under your hair. But for
fun, rotate the scarf and tie the ends
in a perky bow at your temple.

style tip

Wearing a scarf with a
necklace is too much – it
overwhelms your face. Unless
you choose a really simple
necklace, it looks better if
you wear a scarf alone.

This scarf is
designed to be a
headband. It has a built-in
elastic, so tying the ends
is just for decoration.

Buckle up

Belts do more than hold your clothes to your body. They can draw attention to or minimize your waistline, fool the eye into thinking your torso is longer than it is and add a cool fashion accent to your outfit. If your clothes have belt loops, it's best to pass the belt through them but if you're wearing a top or dress with no defined waistband, you have more options for placing the belt.

It's a cinch

Sling low. Braided leather makes a belt both flexible and chic – great to drape over your hips.

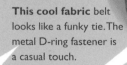

This cool fabric belt looks like a funky tie. The metal D-ring fastener is a casual touch.

A pretty scarf like this one can always double as a belt. Just pass it through the belt loops of your favourite jeans. Crisp fabric will tie in a perky bow too.

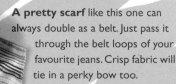

A buckle is like jewellery – key the buckle style (not just the belt colour) to your outfit.

style tip

If you don't want to call attention to your waistline, choose a belt that matches the colour of your outfit. The buckle should be the same colour or have a dull rather than shiny surface.

Pull it together

Thread a sturdy belt through belt loops when your top is tucked into jeans. When your top is outside your jeans, anchor it with a wide or double belt or another interesting style. Tie a pretty woven string belt like a sash over trousers without belt loops.

Try wrapping a ribbon or long scarf around your waist like a belt – or thread it through your belt loops – then use one big pin or a group of little ones to secure it.

Go hand-in-glove

Most gloves are worn for a specific purpose – to keep your hands warm – but that doesn't mean they can't be stylish. Whether you're looking for gloves or mittens, take along the coat, jacket or jumper you'll wear with them so you can choose the right colour and style. There is a wide range of style options available from funky to fun to sweet and even frilly.

Pick a pair

Protect from freezing. For cold weather, choose tailored or sporty insulated gloves.

Cosy posy. Knit and crochet gloves with pretty trims have a sweet, retro style appeal.

Fingerless gloves keep your hands warm and leave your fingertips fully functional.

Gloves with contrasting fingertips are cool and definitely eye-catching.

Wrist warmers are funky and let you show some attitude – they're definitely not for dress-up.

Graceful glamour

Satin gloves are super dressy – for wedding attendants, formal dances and other very fancy events. White and off-white are good choices for any outfit; if you're lucky, you may find a colour to match your outfit. Most styles you'll find are stretchy.

style tip

For gloves, short nails are best. Long or broken nails can be uncomfortable and can damage your gloves.

Style to go

Belts, bags and gloves are important accessories that work hard for you — to secure your jeans, to warm your hands, to carry your gear. But you choose them as much for the way they look as for the way they'll do their job. If you answer "yes" to the following questions, you're making good choices: Does it go with something in your wardrobe? Is it suitable for the time and place you'll wear it? Do you love it? Here are just a few options.

Quilted evening bag

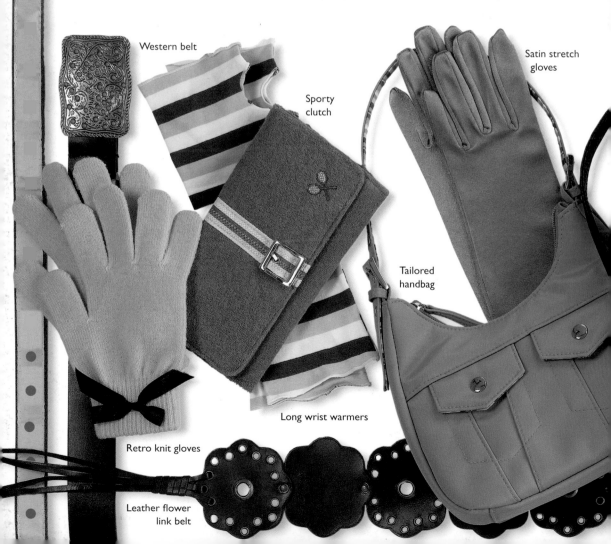

Western belt

Sporty clutch

Satin stretch gloves

Tailored handbag

Long wrist warmers

Retro knit gloves

Leather flower link belt

Beaded tie belt

Sporty
backpack

Satin
handbag

Fingerless
gloves

Canvas handbag

Patterned
shoulder bag

Sequined tote bag

Ribbon belt

Top off your look

Scarves, hats, caps and sunglasses can change the look of an outfit – and that's what makes them fun to choose and wear. They can complement or change the look of your face too, so look in the mirror and let yourself be whomever you see if you like the way she looks. Here are some choices.

1

2

3

4

5

6

1 Long polka-dot scarf
2 Canvas sun hat
3 Knit cap with sequins
4 White and pink sunglasses
5 Wraparound sunglasses
6 Cowgirl hat
7 Turquoise satin scarf
8 Polka-dot scarf
9 Cat's eye sunglasses
10 Retro sunglasses
11 Baseball cap
12 Tinted sunglasses
13 Peaked cap
14 Fedora
15 Pink square sunglasses
16 Long print scarf
17 Frameless sunglasses
18 Long striped scarf
19 Aviator sunglasses

Must-have accessories

Whatever your look is, whichever style is your favourite – or your favourite for today – there are certain accessories you can count on to make you look and feel stylish and you'll always want to have them in your wardrobe. You might choose something with a different style or colour than the examples shown here, but with these top-10 accessories on hand, you're set to be super chic.

1

Big hoops. Simple and classic, plain hoop earrings like these provide a pretty accent that looks great with casual, sporty and semi-dressy clothes. Plus, they're nicely low-key and at the same time big enough to show under longer hair.

2

Super shades. Sunglasses make big statements – pick a pair with the shape, colour, size and personality to match your style.

3

Best bag. Tote your stuff neatly and easily, but with distinction. A sporty style like this keeps you ready for action.

4

Cool watch. Be prompt and pretty with a colourful wristwatch. To avoid the straight and narrow, pick one with interesting strap details and a bold face.

5

Chain bracelet. A loose chain bracelet is incredibly versatile and goes with all but the dressiest clothes in your wardrobe. Choose one like this classic with heart-shaped charm, or pick a different kind of dangle or locket ornament that broadcasts your own style.

6

Bold hairband. A wide hairband looks fabulous so you'll want to let your hair grow if it's really short! They come with bright or quiet colours, big or small patterns and different textures, so you can find one that looks just right with your favourite outfits.

7

Multi-strand bracelet. Delicate but big enough to have character, a multi-strand bracelet adds a grown-up flourish to your wrist.

8

Lovely locket. A long delicate chain necklace with a locket looks sweet and lets you keep a photo or other special little keepsake close – fun to open and show to friends.

9

Fabulous flip-flops. Make them pretty enough to wear on the street – with a big flower or another cool accent – and in a colour you simply love.

10

Pretty posts. Small earrings are simply perfect for everywhere and everyone. Choose glittery or plain, depending on the occasion.

Rosie

Nierah

Alexis

Nikki

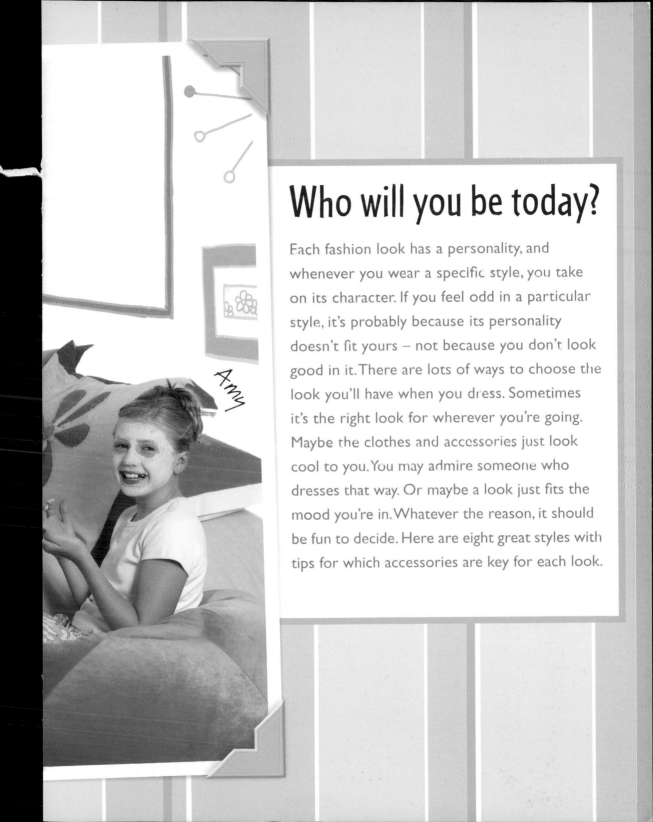

Who will you be today?

Each fashion look has a personality, and whenever you wear a specific style, you take on its character. If you feel odd in a particular style, it's probably because its personality doesn't fit yours – not because you don't look good in it. There are lots of ways to choose the look you'll have when you dress. Sometimes it's the right look for wherever you're going. Maybe the clothes and accessories just look cool to you. You may admire someone who dresses that way. Or maybe a look just fits the mood you're in. Whatever the reason, it should be fun to decide. Here are eight great styles with tips for which accessories are key for each look.

Bohemian girl

Be a free spirit with a very definite sense of style, and take your inspiration from the hippie looks of the 1960s. Go for natural materials – like stone beads, leather and feathers – and artsy details.

Small, rimless or granny-style tinted sunglasses

Short bead dangle necklace

Feather earrings

Crinkly scarf with glittery accents

Tumbled stone and glass bead bracelet sets

Textured leather thong sandals

Western girl

Show your love of the wide, wild West with leather, silver and turquoise and coral accents.

Dangly silver and turquoise earrings

Crushy woven straw cowgirl hat

Turquoise medallion on beaded choker

Leather cuff with stone and silver medallion

Leather belt with silver sutds and silver buckle

Glamour girl

Lavender and rhinestones – what could
be nicer? Indulge your eye for satin,
feathers and glittery trim. Go easy
though, so you look dressed up – not
like you're playing dress-up.

Cats' eye sunglasses
– rosy lenses are nice

Small rhinestone choker

Satin handbag with
gemstone key chain

Super cool boa, made
of fabric or feathers

Surfer girl

So you love the beach and endless sunshine, island prints, shell beads and sea-swept hues? Dress yourself in things that capture the spirit of the waves, the breeze and palm trees – cool bright colours, lots of little beads, waterproof everything.

Tropical print bandana

Aviator shades – blue-tinited

Short, summery shell bead necklace

Sand- and ocean-coloured bead bracelets

Ankle bracelet and matching toe ring

Romantic girl

Soft pretty accessories, things with just a little glitter, pink, and pearls – romantic girls love bows, subtle colours and they don't think twice about wearing frilly accents with jeans and T-shirts – or skirts and jumpers either.

Chiffon scarf

Sweet pearl or silvery bead choker

Pretty watch with ribbon band

Pink glass bead bracelets

Delicate filigree ring

Star athlete

If you live for sports, sport accessories
that can take a bit of action. Go for
fun colours, tough materials and
graphic details like blocky numerals or
footballs. Don't forget, when you're
ready to play, take off things that will
get in your way.

Leather choker with
basketball bead

Colourful backpack with
football motifs and charms

Necklace with player
number dangle

Bright ankle socks with
basketball pompoms

Urban girl

Stroll the streets and visit cafés wearing tough but pretty black and silver accessories. Choose things that are small overall – but just a bit bulky and edgy too, with metal studs and buckles and a bit of sheen and sparkle. Crochet caps look great – keep them on indoors.

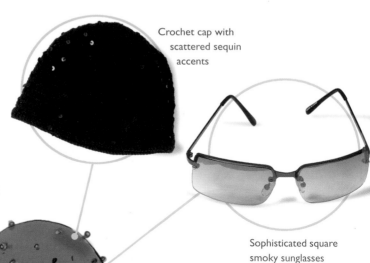

Crochet cap with scattered sequin accents

Sophisticated square smoky sunglasses

Small handbag with pink dice key ring

Chunky chain necklace with dangle

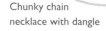

Silver bangles, plain and twisted

Debutante

If your social scene has you mixing, meeting, and greeting, you want to look poised, calm and totally collected. Pick accessories that are ladylike and not too frilly – your look stems from the 1950s and 60s.

Sleek square retro sunglasses

Big, floppy fabric flower pin

Long silky scarf, striped or geometric

Classic watch with coloured face

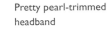

Pretty pearl-trimmed headband

Glossary

Style words to know:

Accessories: Wearable items other than clothes

Bangles: Bracelets without clasps, loose enough to slide on over your hands

Brim: The part of a hat that flares out around your head; it may be large or small, turned up or flared down

Brooch: A large, decorative pin

Cap: A small hat. This word is used for brimless styles, styles with fold-up cuffs, and styles with peaks.

Chandelier earrings: Long earrings that have several tiers of dangling elements

Charm: A small ornament, which often hangs from a bracelet

Chic: Fashionably stylish (this is the French word for style)

Choker: A tight necklace that sits above your collarbone

Crown: The part of a hat that sits over the top of your head, above the brim

Dangles: Hanging earrings more than 2½ centimetres long

Designer: A person who comes up with ideas for accessories, garments, fabrics or other fashion items and oversees their creation

Diva: A star or leading lady; a glamorous style (this is the Greek word for goddess)

Drops: Hanging earrings less than 2½ centimetres long

Ethnic: With style characteristics of a specific culture; usually used to refer to traditional but nonwestern fashions or design elements

Hoops: Wire ring earrings; they may be round, oval, crescent and even square; they sometimes have beads or other ornaments

Hue: Another word for colour

Locket: A hinged pendant that opens to hold a small photo or other keepsake

Look: A combination of clothing and accessories that have particular design features; a specific fashion style

Peak: The stiff oval piece that extends over your forehead on a cap

Pendant: A piece of jewellery that hangs from the centre of a necklace

Posts: Small earrings that sit on your earlobes, without hanging elements

Proportion: Size or dimension, usually used to compare one element to another

Scale: Same as proportion

Studs: This word has several meanings in fashion: 1) post earrings. 2) easily removable, non-sewn buttons used for men's formal shirts (the kind worn with a tuxedo). 3) Small metal ornaments affixed to clothing or jewellery, usually in a decorative pattern.

Style: When used as a noun or adjective, this word can mean a specific fashion look. It can also mean the particular way something is designed, for instance button-down and turtleneck are two collar styles, bell-bottom and boot-cut are two trouser styles. When used as a verb, style means to select and pull-together the pieces of a fashion look or to design individual accessories, garments, fabrics or other fashion items.

Stylish: Having style; usually – but not always – meaning something is currently fashionable

Stylist: A person who selects and pulls together the pieces of a fashion look (usually for photography or television) or who works with a designer to develop the design of individual pieces

Trend: A popular fashion style; trend is usually used to identify or forecast a change in what is fashionable

Index

Acknowledgements

The publisher would like to thank the following for their kind cooperation in the preparation and production of this book:

The fabulous models: Sakura Akiyama-Bowden, Brittany Barbone, Andrea Bloom, Tess Brokaw, Amy Cacciatore, Alexis Carmody, Michelle Chionchio, Mary-Kate Duffy, Kelsey Evenson, Rosie Fodera. Hannah Gross, Nierah Jinwright, Sade Johnson, Maghee Kelsall, Sade Johnson, Juliette Lam, Nikki Lam, Francesca Lobbe, Juliana Merola, Kristin Molinari, and Autumn Stiles…and also their parents, who stuck with us so very patiently at the photo shoot.

Our amazing hairstylists: Azad Desmeropian, Shukran Dogan, Catherine McDermott, Rhondalyn Roberts, John Lisa, and Angela Woodley, for their wonderful skill and dedication.

The super stylists: Maria Stefania Vavylopoulou and Shima Green, for outfitting the girls in the coolest clothes.

Thanks also to Josephine and Katherine Yam at Colourscan for their hard work in bringing it all together; to Nanette Cardon for her work on the index; and of course to the always-glamorous Angela Coppola, Donna Mancini, Cristina Clemente, Nichole Morford, Sharon Lucas, and Gregor Hall for all their help and support.

Hair products used in this book included these products from the L'Oréal Studio Line: Crystal Wax, Out of Bed Whipped Gel, Mega Mousse, Mega Gel, Fast Forward, and Finishing Spray.